A B C **D** E F G H

N O P Q R S T U

Meet big **D** and little **d**.

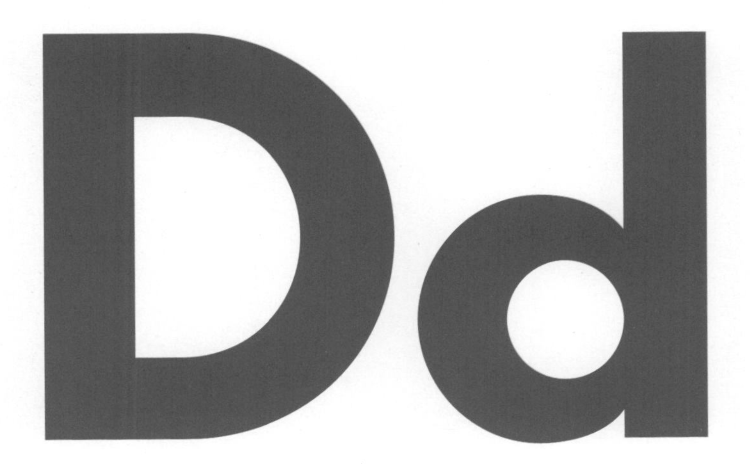

Trace each letter with your finger and say its name.

D is for

dog

D is also for

deer

donut

dig

dive

Dd Story

This is **D**an.
Dan is a **d**og.

Dan **d**ashes with a **d**eer...

and **d**evours a **d**ozen **d**onuts.

Dan **d**igs and **d**igs and **d**igs
in the **d**irt.

Run, jump, **d**unk!
Dan **d**ives into a tub.

Then, **D**an plays with his **d**ucky.
Scrub-a-**d**ub-**d**ub!